The First
Easter

ISBN 0-8249-4155-1

Printed and bound in Mexico by R.R. Donnelley & Sons.

Published by CandyCane Press,
an imprint of Ideals Publications Incorporated
535 Metroplex Drive, Suite 250
Nashville, TN 37211

CIP data on file.

Publisher: Patricia A. Pingry
Designer: Eve DeGrie
Copy Editor: Kristi Richardson

10 8 6 4 2   3 5 7 9

for Gordon

The First
Easter

written by Nancy Skarmeas
paintings by Leslie Benson

An Imprint of Ideals Publications Incorporated
Nashville, Tennessee

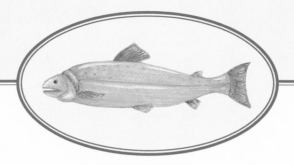

A very long time ago in a land called Judea, there was a man named Jesus. He was the Son of God born on earth. Jesus was a kind and gentle person who did many wonderful things. When he was about thirty years old, Jesus began to teach people about God. He chose twelve men, called disciples, to follow him.

The first disciples that he called, Andrew and Peter, were fishermen. Jesus spoke to them as they cast their nets into the sea. "Follow me," Jesus said, "and I will make you fishers of men." Andrew and Peter, like the other ten, left their work, their families, and their homes to follow Jesus.

Jesus traveled the country with his disciples. He healed the sick, the lame, and the blind. He could even command nature to obey him. One day he and his disciples were sailing. Jesus was tired and went to the back of the boat to sleep. Then a terrible windstorm came up. Great waves rocked the boat, and it began to fill with water. The disciples were afraid the boat would sink. They awakened Jesus and asked for help.

Jesus said to the wind, "Peace, be still." The wind stopped. All was calm.

People were amazed at the miracles that Jesus performed. They began to call him the Messiah, which means the Savior.

One spring, Jesus decided to go to the city of Jerusalem. There, he and the disciples prepared a special meal, called the Passover.

Before they began to eat, Jesus told the disciples that one of them would betray him. Each man asked Jesus, "Is it I?" When Judas asked, Jesus answered, "Thou hast said."

Then Jesus blessed the bread and broke it, saying, "This is my body which is given for you: this do in remembrance of me." Then he took a cup, gave thanks, and said, "This is my blood . . . which is shed for many."

The disciples sang a hymn, then went out into the night. This was Jesus' last supper.

Jesus and the disciples walked to a garden called Gethsemane. In the garden, Jesus asked his friends to stand watch while he prayed. Then he walked away, fell to the ground, and said, "O my Father, if it be possible, let this cup pass from me: nevertheless not as I will, but as thou wilt."

Jesus went back to his disciples and found them asleep. He awakened them and said, "Could ye not watch with me one hour?" Then he walked away and prayed the same prayer again. He returned to find his disciples still asleep. Jesus walked away a third time to pray. This time, when he had finished, he awoke his disciples and said, "Rise, let us be going: behold, he is at hand that doth betray me."

As Jesus spoke, the disciple Judas appeared with an army of soldiers carrying swords. Judas walked straight up to Jesus.

"Master," he said and kissed Jesus on the cheek. Immediately, Jesus was surrounded by soldiers. One of the disciples drew his sword to protect Jesus and struck a soldier. But Jesus told him to put away the sword. "All they that take the sword shall perish with the sword," he said.

Jesus told the disciples that he could have twelve armies of angels to defend him if he but prayed for them. He did not call on the angels, because the Scriptures had promised that the Savior would be betrayed into the hands of his enemies. The soldiers led Jesus away.

After Jesus was led away, Judas knew that he had done something terrible. He had gone to the leaders of Jerusalem and offered to take them to Jesus for a reward of thirty pieces of silver. He said he would betray Jesus with a kiss.

But now Judas was sorry that he had brought the soldiers to Jesus. He had been one of Jesus' beloved disciples, but his greed had made him choose money over his master. Just as Jesus had said, Judas had betrayed him into the hands of his enemies. After Jesus was arrested, Judas got his money, but it couldn't make up for what he had done. He threw the money on the ground.

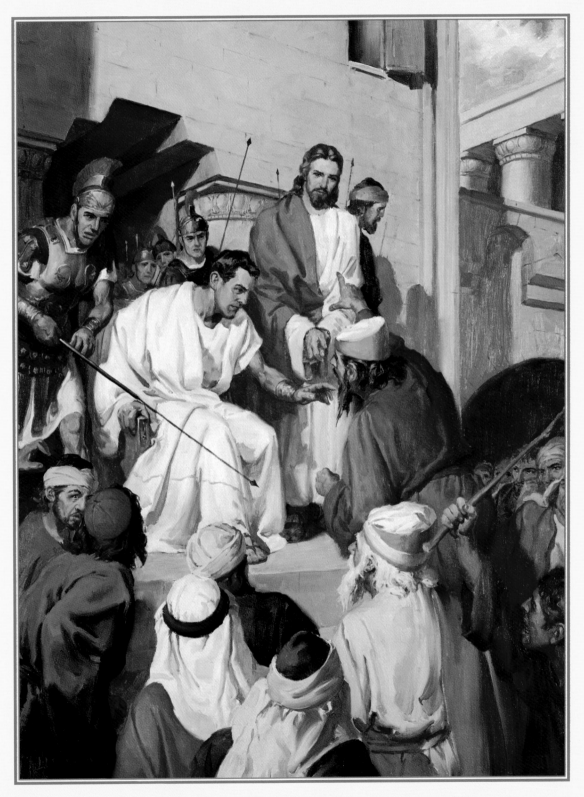

The soldiers brought Jesus to a powerful man named Caiaphas, who asked him, "Are you the Christ, the Son of God?" Jesus answered, "I am."

Caiaphas did not believe Jesus.

The next morning, Jesus was taken to Pontius Pilate, the governor of Jerusalem, who sentenced Jesus to be crucified. He washed his hands, saying to the people, "I am innocent of the blood of this just person."

The soldiers put a crown of thorns on Jesus' head. Then they gave him a large wooden cross to carry and led him away.

Jesus prayed to God as he carried the cross. "Father, forgive them," he said of the soldiers, "for they know not what they do."

The soldiers took Jesus to a hill called Golgotha and crucified him. They made a sign which read THE KING OF THE JEWS and nailed it over his head.

Two thieves were also crucified, one on each side of Jesus. One asked Jesus why God didn't rescue him. But the other asked only that Jesus remember him in heaven. Jesus answered the second thief, "Today shalt thou be with me in paradise."

The sky grew dark as Jesus suffered on the cross. He prayed to his Father. After many hours, he cried out, "My God, my God, why hast thou forsaken me?" Then he died. At that very moment there was a great earthquake, and one of the guards said, "Truly this man was the Son of God."

Jesus' friends took his body from the cross and laid it lovingly in a tomb. Some of Pilate's soldiers sealed the tomb with a great stone, because they had heard the people say that Jesus would rise from the dead after three days.

On Sunday morning, the third day after Jesus' death, two women, both named Mary, went to his tomb. They saw that the stone had been rolled away, and they were frightened. As the women stepped into the tomb, they saw an angel in a long white robe.

The angel told them not to be afraid. Jesus had arisen, as he said he would.

Jesus' friend Mary Magdalene stood at the tomb alone. She was crying because Jesus was gone. A man spoke to her. "Woman, why weepest thou?" he said. Mary thought the man was the gardener and asked him if he knew what had happened to the body in the tomb. The man said "Mary" softly and she knew it was Jesus. "Master," she answered.

Jesus told Mary to find the disciples and tell them he was not dead but was going to heaven to be with the Father. Mary ran quickly to spread the joyous news.

After the women told the disciples the good news, two men were walking toward the village of Emmaus. They were talking about Jesus. The men were sad, because they had loved Jesus and believed he was the Son of God. Suddenly, a third man was walking with them. The stranger asked why they were sad. They told him that Jesus had been crucified.

Then the stranger spoke to them about God. He reminded them that Jesus promised that on the third day after death he would arise. The men's spirits lifted. They soon realized that this stranger beside them was Jesus himself. But when they turned to speak to him, Jesus had disappeared.

The disciples were sharing a meal together when Jesus appeared to them. They wondered how it could be that he was with them again.

"Peace be unto you," Jesus said to them. He held out his hands. The disciples saw the wounds from the cross and knew that it was Jesus. They rejoiced.

But the disciple Thomas was not there to see Jesus. The other men told Thomas they had seen Jesus, but he did not believe them. "Only when I touch the wounds in his hands," said Thomas, "will I believe." When Jesus appeared again, he stood before Thomas and held out his hands. Thomas touched them and said, "My Lord and my God." Jesus answered, "Thomas, because thou hast seen me, thou hast believed; blessed are they that have not seen, and yet have believed."

Many times, Jesus had told his disciples and his friends that after he died he would go to heaven. They couldn't understand this. They thought that death was the end. But they loved Jesus and wanted to believe what he told them.

After he arose from the tomb, Jesus met the disciples on a mountaintop. "All power is given unto me in heaven and in earth," he said. Then he commanded them to spread his teachings throughout the world. "Go ye therefore, and teach all nations," Jesus said, "baptizing them in the name of the Father, and of the Son, and of the Holy Ghost." Jesus told the disciples to take comfort. "I am with you alway," he said, "even unto the end of the world."

The disciples did as Jesus asked. From that day forward, they traveled the world teaching about Jesus. The most wonderful story they told was that of the very first Easter, when Jesus arose from the grave to be with his Father in heaven.

Today, Jesus is called the Good Shepherd. Like a loving shepherd caring for his flock, Jesus cares for all people. On that first Easter long ago, Jesus gave up his life on earth to bring a promise of new life to the world's people. In heaven, by his Father's side, he keeps watch over us all.

SCRIPTURE REFERENCES
for Further Reading

Page 5:
Matthew 4:17–22
Mark 1:14–20; 3:13–19
Luke 3:23; 4:14; 6:13–17
John 1:34

Page 6:
Matthew 4:23–24; 8:23–27
Mark 2:1–12; 4:35–39
Luke 6:17–19
John 1:40–42; 2:1–11; 9:1–7

Page 9:
Matthew 20:17; 26:17,
20–30
Mark: 14:17–26
Luke 22:13–23, 39
John 13:1–2

Page 10:
Matthew 26:36–46
Mark 14: 32–42
Luke 22:40–46
John 15:15; 18:1

Page 13:
Matthew 26:47–57
Mark 14:43–50
Luke 22:47–54
John 18:2–13

Page 14:
Matthew 26:14–16, 48;
27: 3–5
Mark 14:10–11, 44

Page 17:
Matthew 26: 57, 63–66;
27:1–2, 11, 22–24, 29
Mark 14:53–64; 15:1–20
Luke 22:66–71; 23:1–26, 34
John 18:13–24, 28–40; 19:1–17

Page 18:
Matthew 27:33–54
Mark 15:22–39
Luke 23:33–47
John 19:17–30

Page 21:
Matthew 27:55–66; 28:1–6
Mark 15:40–46; 16:1–6
Luke 23:49–56; 24:1–9
John 19:38–42

Page 22:
Mark 16:9–11
John 20:11–18

Page 25:
Luke 24:10–31

Page 26:
Mark 16:14
Luke 24:33–40
John 20:19–29

Page 29:
Matthew 28:16–20

Page 30:
Mark 16:19–20